Contents

What is an ocean?

An ocean is a big body of salt water. Plants and animals live in oceans.

Their homes are called habitats.

Most homes are in water.

Some are on shore.

The shore

Waves roll in.

Crabs hide in the sand.

Birds hunt.

ghost crab

Waves roll out.

Starfish hold

on to rocks.

The open ocean

The sun warms the open ocean.

Kelp grows.

Fish live in the kelp.

kelp

13

Seals eat the fish.

Sharks hunt.

leopard shark

The deep sea

The deep sea is cold
and dark.
Big whales dive here.

sperm whale

It is hard to see in the dark.

Some animals grow big eyes.

Others glow!

jellyfish

The waves roll in and out.

Life is on the move in the ocean.

Glossary

crab sea animal with a wide, flat shell and two front claws

deep sea bottom of the ocean where it is cold and dark

habitat home of a plant or animal

kelp big, brown plant that grows in the ocean

open ocean top of the ocean, far from land

shore part of the ocean where the water ends and the land begins

starfish sea animal that has five arms and is shaped like a star

Read more

i-SPY at the Seaside: What can You Spot? (Collins Michelin i-SPY Guides), i-SPY (Collins, 2016)

Little Kids First Big Book of the Ocean (National Geographic Little Kids), Katherine D Hughes (National Geographic Kids, 2013)

Oceans (Eyewonder), DK (DK Children, 2015)

Websites

www.bbc.co.uk/education/clips/zx676sg

www.ducksters.com/geography/oceans.php

www.theschoolrun.com/homework-help/coastal-habitats

Index